SRA TECH KNOWLEDGE

Step-by-Step Lessons

- Computer Basics
- Keyboarding
- Word Processing
- Drawing and Graphics
- Gadgets
- Presentation
- Spreadsheet
- Database
- Electronic Reference
- Internet

MaryJo Fante Milburn, M.Ed.
Instructional Technology Specialist
Jefferson County Public Schools
Louisville, Kentucky

SRA

Columbus, OH • Chicago, IL • Redmond, WA

The **McGraw·Hill** Companies

Macintosh® and Appleworks® are trademarks of Apple Computer®, Inc., registered in the U.S. and other countries.

Microsoft® and Windows® are registered trademarks of Microsoft Corporation®.

All product names are trademarks of their respective owners.

Windows and Microsoft screen shots reprinted by permission from Microsoft Corporation.

Appleworks and Macintosh screen shots reprinted by permission of Apple Computer, Inc.

PAWS™ copyright © 2004 by SRA/McGraw-Hill.

Photo credits:

1-2, ©Corbis/Bettmann; **3(t),** Courtesy of IBM Corporation, **(b),** ©Corbis/Owen Franken; **4,** ©Corbis; **5(bl),** ©Arthur Tillely/FPG International, **(br),** ©Corbis; **76,** ©First Image.

www.sra4kids.com

Send all inquiries to:
SRA/McGraw-Hill
4400 Easton Commons
Columbus, OH 43219

Printed in the United States of America.

ISBN 0-07-584352-8

6 7 8 9 WEB 08

Contents

History of Computers 1

Computer Safety and Ethics 5

UNIT 1 Computer Basics

LESSON 1 **Parts of a Computer** 8

LESSON 2 **Computer Do's and Don'ts** 9

LESSON 3 **Use the Mouse** 10

LESSON 4 **Use the Keyboard** 11

LESSON 5 **Open and Close a File** 12

LESSON 6 **Open and Close a Program** 13

UNIT 1 Test Part 1 Performance Assessment 14

UNIT 1 Project Complete Rhymes 15

UNIT 2 Keyboarding

LESSON 7 **Find A B C D E F** 17

LESSON 8 **Find G H I J K L** 18

LESSON 9 **Find M N O P Q R** 19

LESSON 10 **Find S T U V W X Y Z** 20

LESSON 11 **Find the Number Keys** 21

LESSON 12 **Find the Symbol Keys** 22

LESSON 13 **Proper Position** 23

LESSON 14 **Return or Enter Key** 24

LESSON 15 **Space Bar** 25

LESSON 16 **Home Keys** 26

LESSON 17 **Home Keys Practice** 27

LESSON 18 **Key Words** 28

UNIT 2 Test Part 1 Performance Assessment 29

UNIT 2 Project Explain a Picture 30

Contents

UNIT 3 Word Processing

LESSON 19 Navigation 32
LESSON 20 Key Text 33
LESSON 21 New Lines 34
LESSON 22 Shift and Caps Lock 35
LESSON 23 Space Bar 36
LESSON 24 Word Wrap 37
LESSON 25 Delete Text 38
LESSON 26 Word Processing Practice 39
LESSON 27 Undo 40
LESSON 28 Special Keys 41
LESSON 29 Highlight Text 42
LESSON 30 Use a Word Processor 43

UNIT 3 Test Part 1 Performance Assessment 44
UNIT 3 Project Write a Poem 45

UNIT 4 Drawing and Graphics

LESSON 31 The Paintbrush Tool 47
LESSON 32 The Shape Tools 48
LESSON 33 The Fill Tool 49
LESSON 34 The Spray Can or Airbrush Tool 50
LESSON 35 The Pencil Tool 51
LESSON 36 The Line Tool 52

UNIT 4 Test Part 1 Performance Assessment 53
UNIT 4 Project Create a Pattern 54

Contents

UNIT 5 Gadgets

LESSON 37 **Input and Output Tools** **56**

LESSON 38 **Use a Printer** **57**

UNIT 5 Test Part 1 Performance Assessment **58**

UNIT 5 Project Group Living and Nonliving Things **59**

UNIT 6 Presentation

LESSON 39 **Watch a Slide Show** **61**

LESSON 40 **Make a Title Slide** **62**

UNIT 6 Test Part 1 Performance Assessment **63**

UNIT 6 Project Describe a Set **64**

UNIT 7 Spreadsheet

LESSON 41 **Explore a Spreadsheet** **66**

LESSON 42 **Enter Data** **67**

UNIT 7 Test Part 1 Performance Assessment **68**

UNIT 7 Project Record the Values of Coins **69**

UNIT 8 Database

LESSON 43 **Learn about Databases** **71**

LESSON 44 **Use a Database** **72**

UNIT 8 Test Part 1 Performance Assessment **73**

UNIT 8 Project Study Symbols **74**

Contents

UNIT 9 Electronic Reference

LESSON 45 Use a CD-ROM 76

LESSON 46 Listen to a Story 77

LESSON 47 Play a Game 78

LESSON 48 Find Information 79

UNIT 9 Test Part 1 Performance Assessment 80

UNIT 9 Project Learn about Your State 81

UNIT 10 Internet

LESSON 49 Review a Home Page 83

LESSON 50 Listen to a Story 84

LESSON 51 Watch a Video 85

LESSON 52 Create a Picture 86

LESSON 53 Play a Game 87

LESSON 54 URLs 88

UNIT 10 Test Part 1 Performance Assessment 89

UNIT 10 Project Answer Questions 90

Glossary R1

Index R7

Mini-Manual R11

History of Computers

No one person invented the computer. There were many inventions over hundreds of years that led to the computers we know today.

People in ancient China, the Middle East, and Greece used the abacus to add and subtract large numbers.

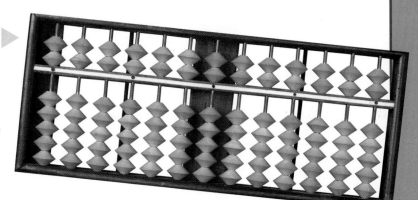

About 185 years ago Charles Babbage tried to make a calculator that would use steam to make it work.

About 135 years ago C.L. Sholes invented a typewriter. It had keys that are like the ones on computer keyboards.

UNIT 10 Project

Science

Use Technology to . . .
Answer Questions

Identify the Problem

1. Answer the question "How do birds fly?"

Collect Data

2. Key the following URL in the location or address box: *www.enchantedlearning. com.*

3. Click **Go** to open the Web page. View the Web page.

4. Click **Birds.** Read the information about flying.

5. Click other links.

Solve the Problem

6. Explain to the class one thing that helps birds fly.

7. Explain to the class whether you think the Web site helped you to learn about birds.

8. Use a draw program to draw a picture of a bird flying.

9. Save and print your picture.

10. Fill out the **Project Scorecard.**

About 115 years ago ▼
Herman Hollerith invented a type of calculator. It stored numbers on punched cards. For more than fifty years, computers continued to use punched cards.

◀ **About 60 years ago** a computer called the ENIAC was built in the United States. The computer was longer and weighed more than a semi truck and trailer. In two hours the ENIAC could do as much as 100 scientists could do in a year.

Performance Assessment

UNIT 10 Test: Part 1

Follow these steps to show what you learned in this unit.

1. Look at a Web site with games.

2. Find a game you like. Open it.

3. Start the game and play it.

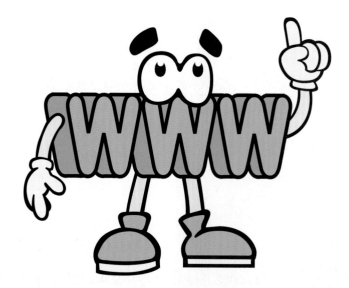

About 45 years ago factories and other very large businesses began to use computers. Many of them cost more than one million dollars.

About 35 years ago the Internet was created. For many years only a few computers were part of the Internet.

About 25 years ago personal computers were invented. These were smaller machines that fit on a desk. Many people in offices, schools, and homes began to use computers. They were less expensive.

LESSON 54
URLs

Follow these steps to go to a Web page.

1. Look at the Web page below. What is the Web page about?

2. Find the Location or Address box. Type the URL that your teacher gives you. The URL is a Web address.

3. Press **Go**, return , or enter to go to the Web page. Tell what you see.

Florida Panther Net

File Edit View Go Bookmarks Help

Back ▾ | Forward ▾ | Stop | Refresh | Home | Search | Print

URL | http: //www.panther.state.fl.us/

Quick Facts
Panthers may only eat once a week

overview   feedback   links   credits

Site Map
Handbook
Natural History
Habitat
Threats
Conservation

Welcome to Florida Panther Net where you can learn about our state animal, the elusive endangered Florida panther. At your fingertips is a rich store of knowledge about the panther, its habitat and the fascinating plants and animals that share its southwest Florida home. Panther Net is a project of the Florida Game and Fresh Water Fish Commission's Advisory Council on Environmental Education. Panther Net is brought to you through proceeds from the Florida panther license plate.

0% of 36k

USE IT!

You can use the Internet to find out about many things.

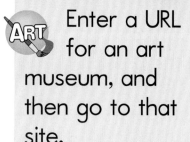
EXTRA CREDIT

ART Enter a URL for an art museum, and then go to that site.

About 20 years ago the computer mouse was introduced. The mouse made personal computers easier to use.

About 15 years ago links were added to the Internet. Links let users click to find more information. This system became known as the World Wide Web.

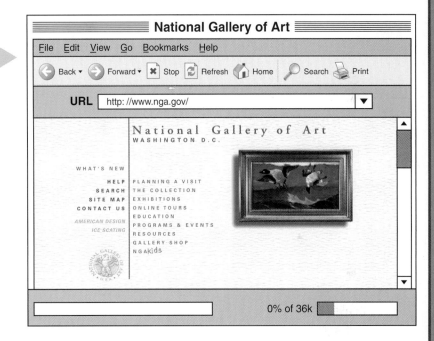

| National Gallery of Art |
| File   Edit   View   Go   Bookmarks   Help |

Back ▾   Forward ▾   ✖ Stop   ↻ Refresh   🏠 Home   🔍 Search   🖨 Print

URL   http: //www.nga.gov/   ▾

National Gallery of Art
WASHINGTON D.C.

WHAT'S NEW

HELP   PLANNING A VISIT
SEARCH   THE COLLECTION
SITE MAP   EXHIBITIONS
CONTACT US   ONLINE TOURS
EDUCATION
AMERICAN DESIGN   PROGRAMS & EVENTS
ICE SCATING   RESOURCES
GALLERY SHOP
NGAkids

0% of 36k

About 15 years ago multi-media computers with CD-ROM drives began to sell in large numbers. CD-ROMs hold a lot more information than floppy disks. They have more room for graphics, video, and sound.

LESSON 53

Play a Game

Follow these steps to play a game.

1. Select a game to play.

2. Click to start the game.

3. Read the directions to play the game.

4. Follow the directions to play the game.

5. Close the game when you are finished.

 **USE IT!**

You can play games on the Web to help you learn things.

 **EXTRA CREDIT**

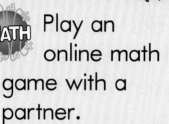 Play an online math game with a partner.

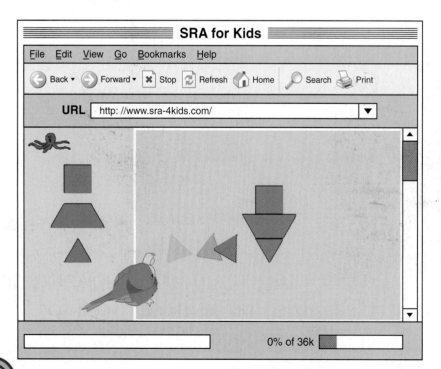

SRA for Kids

File Edit View Go Bookmarks Help

Back ▾   Forward ▾   ✗ Stop   ⟳ Refresh   🏠 Home   🔍 Search   🖨 Print

URL http://www.sra-4kids.com/ ▼

0% of 36k

Computer Safety and Ethics

Computers make it easy to use and share information. You can use computers to talk to people all over the world.

Learn your school's rules for using computers. Rules help you take care of the computer and stay safe. Talk about rules for computers at home.

Respect property

Treat the computer and disks carefully. Keep food and drinks away from them. Ask for help if you do not know how something works. Report problems to people in charge.

Respect privacy

Do not look in other people's files without permission.

Do not delete computer files or programs that belong to other people. Do not change or destroy other people's work.

LESSON 52
Create a Picture

Follow these steps to create a picture.

1. Click the screen to start a new picture.

2. Click a tool to select it.

3. Click a color from the palette.

4. Click the white space and move the mouse to draw.

5. Try the other tools.

 **USE IT!**

You can create artwork on the Web and print it.

 **EXTRA CREDIT**

 SOCIAL STUDIES Draw a picture of a house and print it. Your teacher will help you put a label on it.

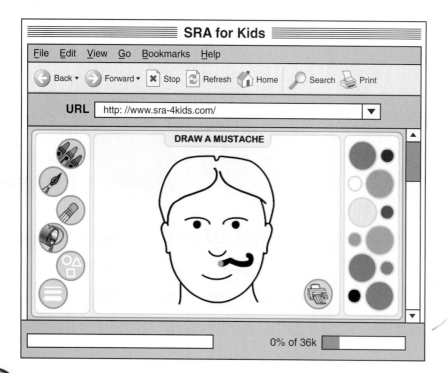

SRA for Kids

File   Edit   View   Go   Bookmarks   Help

Back ▾   Forward ▾   ✖ Stop   ⟳ Refresh   🏠 Home   🔍 Search   🖨 Print

URL   http: //www.sra-4kids.com/   ▼

DRAW A MUSTACHE

0% of 36k

Respect ownership

People's ideas belong to them. If you copy other people's words or pictures without permission, you are stealing from them. Always tell where you got the information.

Keep personal information to yourself

You know not to tell strangers your name, address, or phone number. Do not give out personal information over the Internet either. You may not know to whom you are talking.

Do not tell your name, address, or phone number unless a parent or teacher approves. Tell an adult if someone asks you for personal information or makes you feel uneasy.

Use the Internet for approved purposes

Anyone can create a Web page. Some Web pages contain good information. Others contain wrong information. Some Web pages are not for children. Go to the Web pages your school and home allow.

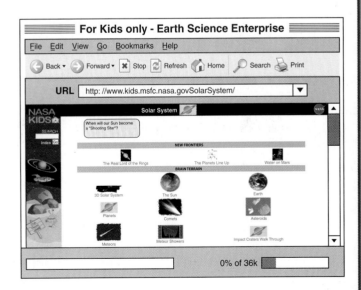

LESSON 51
Watch a Video

Follow these steps to watch a video on the Web.

1. Click to play the video.

2. Watch the video on the screen.

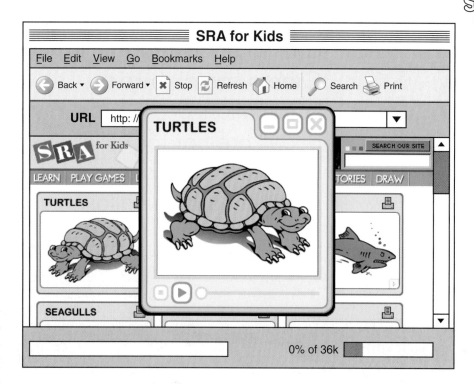

 **USE IT!**

You can watch a video on the Web.

EXTRA CREDIT

SCIENCE Watch a video on the Web about animals. Describe something you saw in the video to a classmate.

Computer Basics

A computer is a machine. It has a memory.

People who work in offices use computers to write letters. Computers in stores keep track of what the store sells.

You can key your name and sentences on a computer. You also can use a computer to draw pictures.

VIEW IT! In this unit you will learn the names of computer parts. You will learn how to take care of a computer.

LESSON 50

Listen to a Story

Follow these steps to listen to a story.

1. Look at the words and pictures on the screen.

2. Click to play the story.

3. Follow the storyteller. Look at the pictures as you listen.

 **USE IT!**

You can listen to a story on the Web.

 EXTRA CREDIT

 Listen to a story on the Web. Tell a classmate about the story you heard.

SRA for Kids

File   Edit   View   Go   Bookmarks   Help

Back ▼   Forward ▼   ✖ Stop   ⟳ Refresh   🏠 Home   🔍 Search   🖨 Print

URL   http: //www.sra-4kids.com/   ▼

SRA for Kids   SEARCH OUR SITE

LEARN | PLAY GAMES | LOOK AT PICTURES | WATCH MOVIES | READ STORIES | DRAW

PANDA BAND   **NAN'S FAMILY**   **MORE STORIES...**
                                                  FIND MORE STORIES
                                                  THAT INTEREST YOU!

                                                  Select a Topic: ◆

                                                  Select a Stories: ◆

                                                                    SEARCH

THIS OLD MAN   **RED RIDING HOOD**   This Day in History
                                                  October 9, 1855

0% of 36k

LESSON 1

Parts of a Computer

Follow these steps to identify the parts of a computer.

1. Point to the monitor.

2. Point to the keyboard.

3. Point to the mouse.

4. Point to a disk drive.

5. Point to the printer.

6. Computer parts are connected with cables. Look for cables.

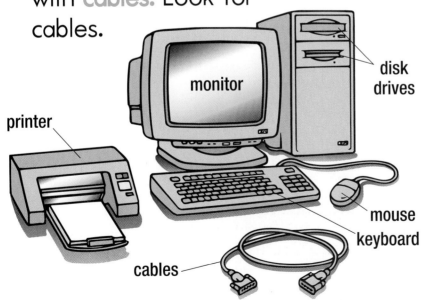

printer

monitor

disk drives

mouse

keyboard

cables

 **USE IT!**

You can learn the names of the parts of a computer so that you can talk about them.

EXTRA CREDIT

 abc LANGUAGE ARTS

Match the names of the computer parts with their pictures.

LESSON 49
Review a Home Page

Follow these steps to review a home page on the Web.

1. Look at the words and pictures on the screen. These make up a Web page.

2. Use the Scroll Bar to move the page.

3. Tell what the Web page is about.

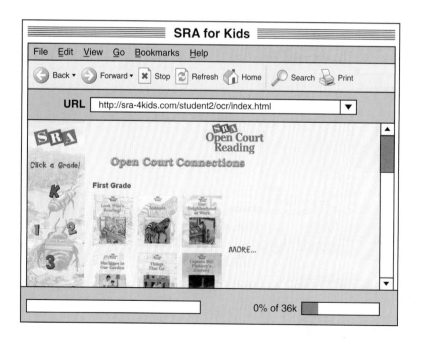

 **USE IT!**

You can find out about lots of things on Web pages.

 **EXTRA CREDIT**

SOCIAL STUDIES View a Web page about farms and describe what you see.

LESSON 2

Computer Do's and Don'ts

Follow these steps to take care of your computer.

1. Insert a floppy disk into the floppy disk drive. Eject the disk.

2. Insert a CD-ROM into the CD-ROM drive. Eject it.

3. Learn how to care for your disks.

4. Follow safety rules. These will protect you and your computer.

 **USE IT!**

You can take proper care of your computer to make it last longer.

EXTRA CREDIT

 Insert a CD-ROM that has a picture saved on it. Then eject it.

Internet

The Internet shows information on the computer.

People in offices use the Internet to find facts to help their businesses grow.

You can use the Internet to find facts about interesting people.

VIEW IT!

In this unit you will learn about many things on the Internet.

LESSON 3

Use the Mouse

Follow these steps to use the mouse.

1. Put your hand over the mouse.

2. Move the mouse around the mouse pad. Watch the cursor  move on the Desktop.

3. Move the cursor to an icon.

4. Click the mouse button. Then click on the background.

5. Click and hold the mouse button on an icon. Move the mouse to drag the icon. Let go of the mouse button.

USE IT!

You can use the mouse to tell the computer what to do.

EXTRA CREDIT

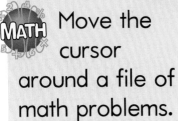 Move the cursor around a file of math problems.

UNIT 9 Project

Social Studies

Use Technology to . . .
Learn about Your State

Understand the Problem

1. What is the geography of your state? You will use a CD-ROM to find out.

2. Load and start the CD-ROM that your teacher gives you.

Gather Information

3. Think of something that you'd like to know about the geography of your state.

4. Click Search.

5. Type in the key word that names what you want to find out about your state.

6. Explore the information on the CD-ROM.

Communicate Your Answer

7. Close the program and eject the CD-ROM.

8. Share what you learned with the class.

9. Fill out the **Project Scorecard.**

Computer Basics

LESSON 4

Use the Keyboard

Follow these steps to use the keyboard.

1. Tap the Arrow keys to move the cursor around the poem.

⬅️ ⬆️ ⬇️ ➡️

2. Move the cursor to the Scroll Bar at the right. Click the up and down arrows. The words move up and down.

3. Move the cursor to the end of the poem. Click the mouse button. Press ⌷return⌷ or ⌷enter⌷.

4. Key your first name.

 **USE IT!**

You can use keys and the mouse to move within a document.

 **EXTRA CREDIT**

 LANGUAGE ARTS Use the Scroll Bar to move up and down in a story.

Electronic Reference

UNIT 9 Test: Part 1

Follow these steps to show what you learned in this unit.

1. Open the CD-ROM drive.

2. Insert the CD-ROM your teacher gives you.

3. Start the CD-ROM program.

4. Tell the teacher what kind of information you found on the CD-ROM.

5. Close the program. Eject the CD-ROM.

Computer Basics

LESSON 5

Open and Close a File

Follow these steps to open and close a file.

1. Move the cursor to the icon named *Open Me.* The icon stands for a file.

2. Double-click the icon.

3. Click the mouse after the last word in the file. Press `return` or `enter`.

4. Key your first name.

5. Click the **Close** box or button to close the file.

 **USE IT!**

You can open a file to make changes to it.

EXTRA CREDIT

 Open a file of insect facts. Then close the file.

LESSON 48
Find Information

Follow these steps to find information on a CD-ROM.

1. Start the CD-ROM.

2. Think of something you want to learn about.

3. You can use a key word to help you search for information. A key word is the topic you want to find.

4. Find **Search** and click it.

5. Type in the key word. Click **Go** or **Find.**

6. Explore the information.

USE IT!

You can use a CD-ROM to find out about things that interest you.

EXTRA CREDIT

SCIENCE Load and find information on a CD-ROM about weather.

LESSON 6

Open and Close a Program

Follow these steps to open and close a program.

1. Double-click the icon for your word processing program.

2. Watch as a blank file opens.

3. Key the words that your teacher tells you.

4. Close the file. Do not save the changes.

5. Quit the program.

 **USE IT!**

You can open many kinds of programs.

EXTRA CREDIT

SOCIAL STUDIES Open a word processing program and key the word *MAP*.

LESSON 47
Play a Game

Follow these steps to play a game on a CD-ROM.

1. Start the CD-ROM.

2. Click the game you want to play.

3. Play the game.

4. Close the program. Eject the CD-ROM.

 **USE IT!**

You can play a game on a CD-ROM during your free time.

 **EXTRA CREDIT**

 Load a CD-ROM and play a spelling game. Tell a friend or the teacher about the game.

Computer Basics

Performance Assessment

UNIT 1 Test: Part 1

Follow these steps to show what you learned in this unit.

1. Insert a floppy disk.

2. Double-click the icon for your word processing program.

3. When a new file opens, key your name and age into it.

4. Close the file and quit the program.

5. Eject the disk.

14   **Performance Assessment • Unit 1 Test: Part 1 Computer Basics**

LESSON 46
Listen to a Story

Follow these steps to listen to a story on a CD-ROM.

1. Start the CD-ROM.

2. Click the story title or the Read the Story icon.

3. Listen to the story.

4. Close the program. Eject the CD-ROM.

 **USE IT!**

You can listen to a story on a CD-ROM during reading time.

EXTRA CREDIT

SOCIAL STUDIES Load and listen to a CD-ROM that has stories about the United States.

UNIT 1 Project

**Reading/Language Arts
Expository Writing**

Use Technology to . . .
Complete Rhymes

Idea

1. Which words rhyme with the names of computer parts and actions?

Organize

2. Open the file named *Rhymes* on the Desktop.

Draft

3. Read the first riddle. Find the rhyming words in the box that complete the riddle.

4. Key the words into the blank.

5. Use the arrow keys to move to the second riddle. Find and key the words that complete the second riddle.

6. Use the arrow keys to move to the third riddle. Find and key the words that complete the third riddle.

7. Save and print your work.

8. Close the file and program.

9. Fill out the **Project Scorecard.**

LESSON 45
Use a CD-ROM

Follow these steps to use a CD-ROM.

1. Press the button to open the CD-ROM drive. Insert the CD-ROM.

2. Press the button again to close the drive.

3. Double-click the icon for the CD-ROM to open the program. What do you see? What kind of information would you find on the CD-ROM?

4. Close the program. Eject the CD-ROM.

 **USE IT!**

You can use a CD-ROM to find information.

 EXTRA CREDIT

 SCIENCE Load and look at a science CD-ROM. Then eject it.

Keyboarding

Keyboarding is typing letters and words on a computer keyboard.

The school office uses keyboarding to key the names of students.

You can use keyboarding to key your name for your teacher.

VIEW IT!

In this unit you learn how to sit properly when you key. You will use the Space Bar, Return or Enter key, and Home keys. You will practice keying words.

TRACKER

UNIT 9

Electronic Reference

Electronic reference is information that is stored on a CD-ROM or on the Internet.

Teachers use electronic references to find answers to questions.

You can use an electronic reference to find the answer to a question.

VIEW IT! In this unit you will learn how to use a CD-ROM to listen to a story, play a game, and find information.

LESSON 7
Find A B C D E F

Follow these steps to learn letters on the keyboard.

1. Look at the keyboard. Find Ⓐ. Tap Ⓐ.

2. Find Ⓑ. Tap Ⓑ.

3. Find Ⓒ. Tap Ⓒ.

4. Find Ⓓ. Tap Ⓓ.

5. Find Ⓔ. Tap Ⓔ.

6. Find Ⓕ. Tap Ⓕ.

7. Practice tapping Ⓐ Ⓑ Ⓒ Ⓓ Ⓔ Ⓕ.

 **USE IT!**

You can use *A, B, C, D, E,* and *F* to key words.

 **EXTRA CREDIT**

 Tap *F, A, C, E* to key the word *FACE.*

UNIT 8 Project

Use Technology to . . .
Study Symbols

Understand the Problem

1. Open the file named *U.S. Symbols.*

2. Look at the database. It has data about some symbols of the United States.

3. Look at the questions about the database. You will use the database to answer the questions.

Gather Information

4. Read the fields in the database. Use the arrow keys to move to each cell as you read.

5. Read the data in each row. Use the arrow keys to move to each cell as you read.

Find a Solution

6. Use the database to find the answer to each question. Write the answers on a piece of paper.

7. Fill out the **Project Scorecard.**

LESSON 8
Find G H I J K L

Follow these steps to learn letters on the keyboard.

1. Look at the keyboard. Find [G]. Tap [G].

2. Find [H]. Tap [H].

3. Find [I]. Tap [I].

4. Find [J]. Tap [J].

5. Find [K]. Tap [K].

6. Find [L]. Tap [L].

7. Practice tapping [G] [H] [I] [J] [K] [L].

 **USE IT!**

You can use *G*, *H*, *I*, *J*, *K*, and *L* to key words.

EXTRA CREDIT

MATH Tap the pattern GGHHIIJJKKLL.

Database

UNIT 8 Test: Part 1

Follow these steps to show what you learned in this unit.

1. Use the Arrow keys to move around the database.

2. Find the name *Aunt Ellen.* In what state does she live?

3. Who lives in Florida?

4. In what city and state does Aunt Jen live?

Name	City	State
Aunt Jen	Denver	Colorado
Aunt Ellen	Stockton	California
Uncle Andrew	Jacksonville	Florida

LESSON 9
Find M N O P Q R

Follow these steps to learn letters on the keyboard.

1. Look at the keyboard. Find M. Tap M.

2. Find N. Tap N.

3. Find O. Tap O.

4. Find P. Tap P.

5. Find Q. Tap Q.

6. Find R. Tap R.

7. Practice tapping M N O P Q R.

 **USE IT!**

You can use *M, N, O, P, Q,* and *R* to key words.

EXTRA CREDIT

SOCIAL STUDIES Tap the first letter of the social studies words *River, North,* and *Ocean.*

LESSON 44
Use a Database

Follow these steps to find information in a database.

1. Open the database file *Favorites.*

2. Use the Arrow keys to move around the database. → ↓ ↑ ←

3. Find the color *blue.* Whose favorite color is blue?

4. Find the person whose favorite color is red and whose favorite fruit is an apple.

Name	Color	Fruit
Ashley	red	pear
Kira	yellow	cherry
Tommy	blue	banana
Taylor	pink	banana
Darren	red	apple

 **USE IT!**

You can find information in a database.

EXTRA CREDIT

SOCIAL STUDIES Find a state capital in the *Cities* database.

LESSON 10
Find S T U V W X Y Z

Follow these steps to learn letters on the keyboard.

1. Look at the keyboard. Find ⑤. Tap ⑤.

2. Find Ⓣ. Tap Ⓣ.

3. Find Ⓤ. Tap Ⓤ.

4. Find Ⓥ. Tap Ⓥ.

5. Find Ⓦ. Tap Ⓦ.

6. Find Ⓧ. Tap Ⓧ.

7. Find Ⓨ. Tap Ⓨ.

8. Find Ⓩ. Tap Ⓩ.

9. Practice tapping ⑤ Ⓣ Ⓤ Ⓥ Ⓦ Ⓧ Ⓨ Ⓩ.

 **USE IT!**

You can use *S, T, U, V, W, X, Y,* and *Z* to key words.

EXTRA CREDIT

ART Tap the first letter of the colors *White, Violet,* and *Yellow.*

S T U V W X Y Z

LESSON 43
Learn about Databases

Follow these steps to learn about databases.

1. Open the file *Books.* This is a database table.

2. The information in the database is kept in records. Each line in the table is a separate record.

3. The headings in the top row are called fields. Databases usually have more than one field.

4. Find the name of the book *Corduroy* and its author.

Book	Author
Amelia Bedelia	Peggy Parish
Bedtime for Frances	Russell Hoban
Corduroy	Don Freeman

 **USE IT!**

You can use a database to list the books you have read.

EXTRA CREDIT

 Find and click the author of *Amelia Bedelia* in the *Books* database.

LESSON 11
Find the Number Keys

Follow these steps to learn numbers on the keyboard.

1. Look at the keyboard. Find the number keys.

2. Tap the number keys:
1 2 3 4 5

3. Tap the number keys:
6 7 8 9 0

4. Practice tapping the number keys.

 **USE IT!**

You can use the number keys to key numbers on a page.

 **EXTRA CREDIT**

 Key the answer to $1 + 3 =$ ____.

Database

A database is an organized group of information.

The school office uses a database to keep track of the names, addresses, and grade levels of students.

You can use a database to keep track of your friends' names and phone numbers.

VIEW IT! In this unit you will look at a database and its parts. You will also find items in a database.

Keyboarding

LESSON 12
Find the Symbol Keys

Follow these steps to learn the symbol keys.

1. Look at the keyboard. Find the symbol keys. Most of them are the same as the number keys.

2. Tap the ⌈shift⌋ key at the same time as the symbol key.

3. Tap each symbol key: `!` `@` `#` `$` `%` `^`.

4. Tap each symbol key: `&` `*` `(` `)` `-` `+`.

5. Practice tapping symbols.

 **USE IT!**

You can use the symbol keys when you write.

EXTRA CREDIT

MATH Key $ and then the number 5 to make $5.

UNIT 7 Project

Math

Use Technology to . . .
Record the Values of Coins

Understand the Problem

1. Open the spreadsheet file named *Coins.*

2. You will enter the data needed to complete the spreadsheet.

Make a Plan

3. Look at the column heads in the spreadsheet.

4. Think of how much each coin is worth.

5. Enter the number value of each coin in the second row of the spreadsheet.

6. Use the arrow keys to move to the third row of the spreadsheet.

7. Enter the value in words for each coin in the third row of the spreadsheet.

8. Save and print your work.

Check Your Answers

9. Add the numbers that you entered in the second row. The sum should be the same as the number in cell F2.

10. Fill out the **Project Scorecard.**

LESSON 13
Proper Position

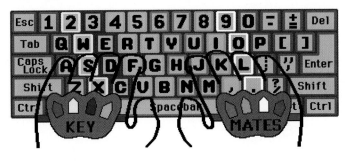

KEY MATES

Follow these steps to get ready to keyboard.

1. Place your fingers on A S D F and J K L :. These are called the Home keys. Curve your fingers.

2. Rest your thumbs lightly on space.

3. Put both feet on the floor. Keep your elbows close to your sides.

4. Tap A and lift up your finger quickly. Practice tapping A.

 **USE IT!**

You can use the Home keys to help find other keys.

EXTRA CREDIT

LANGUAGE ARTS Tap the first letter of the word *Spelling.*

UNIT 7 Test: Part 1

Follow these steps to show what you learned in this unit.

1. Open the spreadsheet *Fruit.*

2. Look at the spreadsheet. Say how many apples there are.

3. What is the cell address of *Oranges?*

4. Click in cell D2. Key the number *5.*

5. Print your work.

	A	B	C	D
1	Apples	Bananas	Oranges	Pears
2	4	6	3	

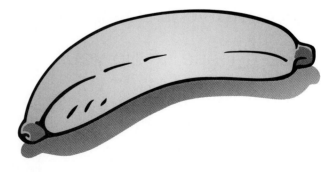

LESSON 14
Return or Enter Key

Learn to use the Return or Enter key.

1. Look at the picture. Place your fingers on the Home keys. Curve your fingers.

2. Find K. Tap K.

3. Tap return or enter with your right little finger.

4. Find D. Tap D. Tap return or enter with your right little finger.

USE IT!

You can use return or enter to move to a new line.

EXTRA CREDIT

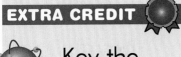

SCIENCE Key the season *FALL*. Press Return or Enter.

Spreadsheet

LESSON 42
Enter Data

Follow these steps to enter data into a spreadsheet.

1. Open the spreadsheet *Food.*

2. Click cell D2 to select it.

3. Key *2.* Press ⌐return⌐ or ⌐enter⌐.

4. Use ⌐↓⌐ and ⌐←⌐ to move to cell B5.

5. Key *4.* Press ⌐return⌐ or ⌐enter⌐.

6. Use ⌐→⌐ to move to cell D5. Key *0.* Press ⌐return⌐ or ⌐enter⌐.

 **USE IT!**

You can key data into a spreadsheet.

EXTRA CREDIT

ART In the spreadsheet about shapes, key the number *1* in cell C3. Press ⌐return⌐ or ⌐enter⌐.

	A	B	C	D	E
1		Pizza	Grilled Cheese	Spaghetti	Egg Rolls
2	Table 1	3	1	2	0
3	Table 2	4	0	1	1
4	Table 3	2	2	1	1
5	Table 4	4	1	0	1

LESSON 15
Space Bar

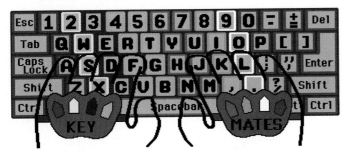

Learn to use the Space Bar.

1. Look at the picture. Place your fingers on the Home keys.

2. Tap [space] with the side of your right thumb. The Space Bar puts spaces between letters and words.

3. Practice tapping [space]. Try to make just one space without looking at the keyboard.

4. Practice tapping a letter and then [space].

 USE IT!

You can use [space] to put a space between words.

 Key
ASK DAD.

LESSON 41
Explore a Spreadsheet

Follow these steps to learn about spreadsheets.

1. Open the file *Stuffed Animals*.

2. Find the letter *A* at the top. From *A* to the bottom is called *column A.* Columns are named across the top.

3. Find the number *1* at the side. This is called *row 1.* Rows are named along the side.

4. Each small box is called a cell.

5. Cell addresses tell where a cell is. They have a letter and a number. Find the word *Brown.* Find the column letter. What is it? Find the row number. What is it? Put the column and row number together to make the cell address. What is it?

 USE IT!

You can use the names of spreadsheet parts to talk about them.

 EXTRA CREDIT

SOCIAL STUDIES View a spreadsheet on how students go to school. Click the cell that says how many students walk to school.

LESSON 16
Home Keys

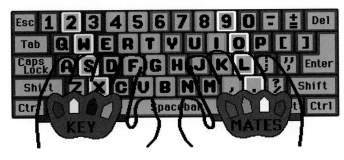

Learn to key the Home keys.

1. Place the fingers of your left hand on ⒜ ⒮ ⒟ and ⒡ .

2. Place the fingers of your right hand on ⒥ ⒦ ⒧ and ⒴ .

3. Practice keying the lines below. Tap [space] when you see a space. Tap [return] or [enter] at the end of each line. Try not to look at the keyboard.

1 A S D F J K L ; ASDF JKL;
2 ; L K J F D S A ;LKJ FDSA

3 ASDF JKL; A S D F J K L ;
4 A S D F J K L ; ASDF JKL;

 **USE IT!**

You can use the Home keys to key words.

EXTRA CREDIT

Key the letter pattern ;A LS KD JF.

Spreadsheet

A spreadsheet works with numbers and words.
It looks like a chart or a table.

School offices use a spreadsheet to add and subtract the number of students in the school and each class.

You can use a spreadsheet to keep track of the number of students in your class.

VIEW IT!

In this unit you will learn about cells, columns, rows, and cell addresses. You will enter data into a spreadsheet.

LESSON 17
Home Keys Practice

KEY MATES

Practice using the Home keys.

1. Look at the picture. Review which finger goes on each Home key.

2. Place the correct fingers on the Home keys.

3. Practice keying the following lines. Reach with your right little finger to tap `return` or `enter`.

1 ASDF JKL; A S D F J K L ;
2 AA DD SS FF JJ LL KK ;;

3 SA FJ LA AF AS AK DK SL
4 JF KD LS DA KL L; S; D;

 **USE IT!**

You can use the Home keys to help find other keys.

EXTRA CREDIT

SOCIAL STUDIES Key the first letter of the states *Kansas, Alabama,* and *Louisiana.*

UNIT 6 Project

Math

Use Technology to . . .
Describe a Set

Understand the Problem

1. Open the presentation named *Math* on your Desktop.

2. You will watch the presentation and then make a new slide.

3. You will key an equation to show how many squares there are in all.

Make a Plan

4. Look at the slide show. Add the red squares plus the blue squares to get a total.

5. Close the slide show.

6. Open the presentation program. Select **Blank Presentation** and choose **Title Only** layout.

7. Key the equation $2 + 3 =$. Complete the equation by keying the answer.

8. Save your slide as *Math Answer.*

Check Your Answer

9. Watch the slide show again to check your answer.

10. Fill out the **Project Scorecard.**

LESSON 18
Key Words

KEY MATES

Practice keying words.

1. Place your fingers on the Home keys.

2. Practice keying the words below. Do not look at the keyboard. Keep your eyes on the book.

1   LAD LAD LASS LASS
2   SAD SAD DAD DAD

3   ADD ADD FALL FALL
4   ALL ALL FAD FAD

 USE IT!

You can use the Home keys to key words.

 EXTRA CREDIT

LANGUAGE ARTS

Key *DAD*, press return or enter, and then key *SAD*.

Performance Assessment

UNIT 6 Test: Part 1

Follow these steps to show what you learned in this unit.

1. Open the presentation program.

2. Make a title slide.

3. Key the title *My Favorite Animal* on the slide.

4. Show the slide to your teacher.

UNIT 2 Test: Part 1

Follow these steps to show what you learned in this unit.

1. Key the lines below.

2. When you are finished, key your name on a new line and print your work.

1 A S D F J K L ; A S D F J K L ;
2 A A S S D D F F J J K K L L ; ;

3 A A J J S S K K D D L L F F ; ;
4 A F S D J K L ; A J S K D L F ;

LESSON 40
Make a Title Slide

Follow these steps to make a title slide.

1. Open the presentation program.

2. Select Blank Presentation.

3. Choose the **Title Only** layout.

4. Click inside the box that says **Click to Add a Title.**

5. Key *PIZZA.*

 **USE IT!**

You can make a title slide to name your slide show presentation.

 **EXTRA CREDIT**

SOCIAL STUDIES Make a title slide called *MY CITY.*

UNIT 2 Project

**Reading/Language Arts
Descriptive Writing**

Use Technology to . . .
Explain a Picture

Idea

1. You can write sentences that tell about a picture.

Organize

2. Use the proper keyboarding position. Open the file named *Pond*.

3. Look at the picture on the screen. There are three animals.

4. Read the sentence below the picture.

Draft

5. Look at the words in the box.

6. Use the words in the box to key a sentence about the green animal.

7. Use the remaining words in the box to key a sentence about the third animal.

8. Save and print your work.

9. Close the file and program.

10. Fill out the **Project Scorecard.**

LESSON 39
Watch a Slide Show

Follow these steps to watch a slide show.

1. Open the document *Mary.*

2. Click **Slide Show.**

3. Move the cursor down and click **View Show.**

4. Click when you are ready to move to the next slide.

5. When the show is over, click the mouse to exit.

 **USE IT!**

You can watch a slide show to read the words of your favorite nursery rhyme.

 EXTRA CREDIT

 Watch a slide show about capital letters, then think of a word that starts with a capital letter.

UNIT 3

Word Processing

Word processing is writing words and sentences on the computer.

People use word processing to write reports and letters. Your teacher can write notes to your parents.

You can key your name and words to give to your teacher.

VIEW IT!

In this unit you will learn how to move around a page, erase words, undo words, use special keys, and highlight words and spaces.

UNIT 6

Presentation

Presentations give people information. Watching a computer presentation is like reading a book except that the words and pictures are on slides instead of pages.

People use presentations when they give reports to people.

You can watch a presentation about a book or poem you have read.

VIEW IT!

In this unit you will watch a slide show and learn how to make a title slide.

60

LESSON 19
Navigation

Follow these steps to practice moving around a page.

1. Open the document *Twinkle, Twinkle.*

2. Find the blinking line. This is the insertion point.

3. Move the cursor before the word *star* in the first line. Click. Key the word *little.* Key one space.

4. Use the Arrow keys and Scroll Bar to move around the document.

 **USE IT!**

You can move the insertion point and add text to a document.

EXTRA CREDIT

 After the number *1*, key a space, then key the number *2.*

UNIT 5 Project

Use Technology to . . .
Group Living and Nonliving Things

Identify the Problem

1. Plan to group names of living and nonliving things into lists that you will print.

Collect Data

2. Open a new word processing file.

3. Key the following words on a line: *bird, fish, rock, spider, sun, tree, water.*

Solve the Problem

4. Find the words that name nonliving things. Key the words in a list.

5. Skip two lines.

6. Find the words that name living things.

7. Key the words in a list.

8. Next to each living thing, key the names of two of its body parts.

9. Save the file as *Science.* Print your document.

10. Fill out the **Project Scorecard.**

LESSON 20
Key Text

Follow these steps to practice keying text into a document.

1. Open the document *Text*.

2. Key the letters *A* through *J*.

3. Key the numbers *0* through *9*.

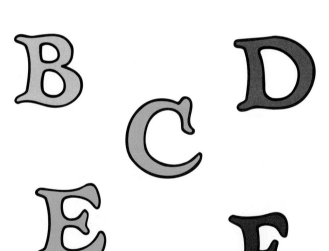

 **USE IT!**

You can key your schoolwork into a word processing document.

 EXTRA CREDIT

 Open the document *Animals* and key the word *BIRD*.

UNIT 5 Test: Part 1

Follow these steps to show what you learned in this unit.

1. Open a new word processing document.

2. Key the word *star*. Press ⟨return⟩ or ⟨enter⟩, and then key the word *moon*.

3. Use the **File** menu to print your document.

4. Give the printed page to your teacher.

LESSON 21
New Lines

Follow these steps to make new lines and blank lines.

1. Open the document *New Lines.*

2. Click after the last word in the document.

3. Press [return] or [enter] three times.

4. Key the name of your favorite animal. Press [return] or [enter].

5. Key the numbers *1, 2,* and *3.* Key each number on a new line.

 **USE IT!**

You can press [return] or [enter] to add new or blank lines to a document.

EXTRA CREDIT

 MATH Key the numbers *5, 6,* and *7.* Key each number on a new line.

Gadgets

LESSON 38
Use a Printer

Follow these steps to print a document using the File menu.

1. Open the word processing document *Food.*

2. Key your favorite breakfast food.

3. Click **File** on the menu bar. Use the mouse to choose **Print** from the **File** menu.

4. Click **Print** or **OK.**

 **USE IT!**

You can create artwork and print it to share with the class.

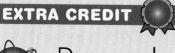 **EXTRA CREDIT**

SCIENCE Draw and print a picture of the moon.

LESSON 22

Shift and Caps Lock

Follow these steps to use the Shift and Caps Lock keys.

1. Open the document *Capitals.*

2. Press and hold shift. Tap A. Release shift.

3. Key the first line that your teacher gives to you. Remember to press return or enter to start a new line.

4. Press caps lock. Key the second line.

 **USE IT!**

You can use shift to key capital letters.

EXTRA CREDIT

SOCIAL STUDIES Key *Dad.* On a new line, key *MOM* in capital letters.

LESSON 37
Input and Output Tools

Follow these steps to learn about input and output tools.

1. Computer gadgets are also called input and output tools.

2. A scanner is an input tool. It can copy words or pictures into the computer. Point to the scanner.

3. A printer is an output tool. It prints words or pictures onto a sheet of paper. Point to the printer.

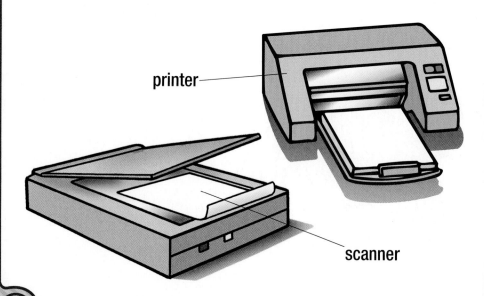

printer

scanner

 **USE IT!**

You can use the real names of input and output tools when you talk about them.

EXTRA CREDIT

SOCIAL STUDIES Key the name of the state in which you live, and then print the document.

LESSON 23

Space Bar

Follow these steps to use the Space Bar.

1. Open the document *Roses.* Look to see that there are no spaces between the words.

2. Move the insertion point after the first five letters. Press space.

3. Put a space between each word.

 **USE IT!**

You can key spaces between words to make them easier to read.

 **EXTRA CREDIT**

 Open the document *Numbers.* Key a space between the numbers.

Gadgets

Input and Output tools are gadgets used to create, edit, and view documents on the computer.

People use input tools to put information into the computer. They use output tools to take the information out.

You can print your homework with a printer and turn it in to your teacher.

VIEW IT!

In this unit you will name different input and output tools and use a printer to share your work with the class.

Word Processing

LESSON 24
Word Wrap

Follow these steps to use word wrap.

1. Open the document *Sheep.*

2. Key the sentences shown below. Do not press ⌜return⌝ or ⌜enter⌝.

> There once was a boy who watched over a flock of sheep. The sheep ate grass in the fields.

3. Did you see what happened after you reached the end of a line? This is called word wrap.

4. Put the insertion point right before the beginning of the second sentence.

5. Key this sentence: *He made sure the sheep were safe.* Did you see the words wrap around the lines as you keyed?

 **USE IT!**

You can use word wrap to save time.

EXTRA CREDIT

 Use word wrap to key the sentence *Plants need water to grow.*

UNIT 4 Project

Art

Use Technology to . . .
Create a Pattern

Begin to Create

1. Think about how you could use drawing and graphics tools to create a repeating pattern.

2. Open a new document in your drawing and graphics program.

3. Use the drawing and graphics tools to experiment with different patterns.

Organize and Design

4. Decide on a pattern that you like.

5. Use the shape tools and the fill tools to make your pattern.

6. You can also use the other tools.

Final Composition

7. Look at your pattern. If there are any mistakes, erase them and redo those parts of the pattern.

8. Save your picture as *Pattern.* Then print it.

9. Exchange patterns with a classmate and tell your classmate what you like about his or her pattern.

10. Fill out the **Project Scorecard.**

LESSON 25
Delete Text

Follow these steps to delete text.

1. Open the document *Franklin.*

2. Move the cursor so that the insertion point is after the last sentence.

3. Tap `delete` or `backspace` seven times. This will delete the quotation marks, the period, the word *wise,* and the space.

4. Hold down `delete` or `backspace` to delete the entire sentence and the blank line above it.

 **USE IT!**

You can delete letters, numbers, spaces, or lines using `delete` or `backspace`.

EXTRA CREDIT

 Open the document *Lambs.* Delete the mistake.

Drawing and Graphics

UNIT 4 Test: Part 1

Follow these steps to show what you learned in this unit.

1. Draw a picture using the Paintbrush tool. Use two colors in the picture.

2. Use a Shape tool and make a shape.

3. Fill the shape with color.

4. Use the Line tool to draw a picture.

5. Use the Eraser tool to erase part of the picture.

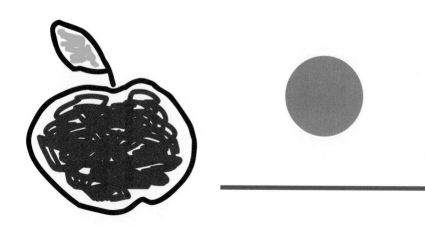

Word Processing

LESSON 26
Word Processing Practice

Follow these steps to practice word processing.

1. Open the document *Practice1*.

2. Key these sentences into your document.

> The ladybug crawled on the ground. Then it made a cocoon. It changed into a butterfly and flew away.

3. Use ⌈return⌉ or ⌈enter⌉ to put each sentence on a different line.

4. Delete the word *ladybug*. Key the word *caterpillar*.

 **USE IT!**

You can use special keys and features to change your words easily.

EXTRA CREDIT

Key the following text: *Mix red with yellow to make orange.*

LESSON 36
The Line Tool

Follow these steps to use the Line tool.

1. Open a new paint document.

2. Click the Line tool . Click a color in the Color Palette.

3. Move the cursor to the white space. Drag to draw a line.

4. Draw your home or school using lines.

 **USE IT!**

You can use the Line tool to draw pictures with straight lines.

EXTRA CREDIT

SCIENCE Using the Line tool, draw a doghouse using three colors.

LESSON 27

Undo

Follow these steps to use Undo.

1. Open the document *Undo.*

2. Key your name at the end of the sentence.

3. Click **Undo** to delete your name.

4. Key the numbers *1* through *9.* Put a space after each number.

5. Click **Undo** to undo your keying.

 **USE IT!**

You can use **Undo** if you change your mind.

EXTRA CREDIT

 Key the numbers *1, 2,* and *4.* Then click **Undo** and key the numbers *1* through *4* correctly.

LESSON 35

The Pencil Tool

Follow these steps to use the Pencil tool.

1. Open a new paint document.

2. Click the Pencil tool .

3. Drag to draw a picture. Move your hand slowly. Use different colors in the Color Palette.

4. If you make a mistake, click the Eraser tool. Drag over the part of the picture you want to erase.

 **USE IT!**

You can make a sketch using the Pencil tool.

EXTRA CREDIT

SOCIAL STUDIES Draw a car using at least three colors.

LESSON 28
Special Keys

Follow these steps to move around a document quickly.

1. Open the document *Story.* Read the first line in the document.

2. Press [page down]. Read the top line. When you press [page down], you move down.

3. Press [page up]. When you press [page up], you move up.

4. Press [end] or [Ctrl]-[end]. What part of the document do you see?

5. Press [home] or [Ctrl]-[home] to return to the beginning.

 **USE IT!**

You can move around a document quickly by using special keys.

EXTRA CREDIT

SOCIAL STUDIES Move to the end of the document about school, then back to the beginning.

LESSON 34

The Spray Can or Airbrush Tool

Follow these steps to use the Spray Can or Airbrush tool.

1. Open a new paint document.

2. Click the Spray Can or Airbrush tool . Click a color in the Color Palette.

3. Move the cursor to the white space. Drag to create a landscape like a forest.

4. Click different colors as you paint.

 **USE IT!**

You can create softer backgrounds for pictures using the Spray Can or Airbrush tool.

EXTRA CREDIT

SCIENCE Use the Spray Can or Airbrush tool to draw a picture of a sunset.

LESSON 29
Highlight Text

Follow these steps to highlight and delete words or lines.

1. Open the document *Diddle.*

2. Move the cursor after the word *mean* and click. Drag back across the word. Press delete or backspace.

3. Highlight and delete the word *big.*

4. Highlight and delete the blank line between the first two lines.

 **USE IT!**

You can erase words and lines by highlighting and deleting.

EXTRA CREDIT

 Open the document *Colors.* Highlight and delete the word *pink.*

LESSON 33

The Fill Tool

Follow these steps to fill a space with color.

1. Open a new paint document.

2. Draw three shapes. Make parts of them cover parts of other shapes ☐ ○ ◁.

3. Click the Fill tool 🪣. Select a color from the Color Palette.

4. Click a shape and watch as it is filled with the color you chose. Fill the other shapes with different colors.

5. Choose a different color. Click the white space. Watch as the background is filled with the color you chose.

 **USE IT!**

You can color large spaces quickly using the Fill tool.

EXTRA CREDIT

SOCIAL STUDIES Use the Shape and Fill tools to draw and color a picture of a friend.

LESSON 30

Use a Word Processor

Follow these steps to practice using word processing skills.

1. Open the document *Practice.*

2. Highlight and delete the sentence *The whale was diving.*

3. Delete the word *him.*

4. Key the word *you.*

5. Put the insertion point before the first word.

6. Key your name. Press `return` or `enter` two times.

 **USE IT!**

You can use word processing skills to help you write your schoolwork.

EXTRA CREDIT

 SCIENCE Open the document *Plants.* Delete the last sentence.

LESSON 32
The Shape Tools

Follow these steps to use the Shape tools.

1. Open a new paint document.

2. Click the Rectangle Shape tool .

3. Move the cursor to the white space. Drag the mouse. Let go when the rectangle is the size you want.

4. Draw more shapes. Click a Shape tool and drag to make a shape ⬭ ◪ .

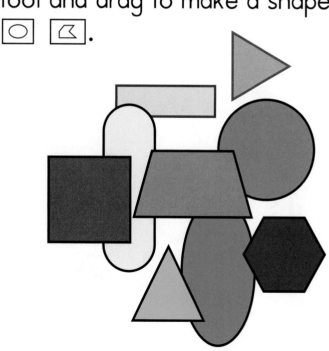

USE IT!

You can use the Shape tools to draw perfect shapes.

EXTRA CREDIT

MATH Use the Rounded Rectangle Shape tool to draw six rounded rectangle shapes.

Word Processing

UNIT 3 Test: Part 1

Follow these steps to show what you learned in this unit.

1. Key the lines below.

> The Butterfly
> The butterfly is blue and black.
> It flies from place to place.

2. Change the word *black* to *yellow*.

3. Undo the change.

4. Move to the top of the document.

5. Key the word *Poem.* Press ⌷return⌷ or ⌷enter⌷ two times.

LESSON 31

The Paintbrush Tool

Follow these steps to use the Paintbrush tool and Color Palette.

1. Open a new paint document.

2. Select the **Paintbrush tool** . Click a color in the Color Palette.

3. Move the cursor to the white space. Create a picture by dragging the mouse.

4. Click another color in the Color Palette.

5. Finish your picture using different colors.

 **USE IT!**

You can make pictures with your computer and give them to people as cards or gifts.

EXTRA CREDIT

Draw a bird's nest using different colors.

UNIT 3 Project

Reading/Language Arts Poetry

Use Technology to . . .
Write a Poem

Idea

1. Plan to write a poem about yourself, and share it with a friend.

Organize

2. Open a new word processing file.

3. Key a list of words that describe yourself.

Draft

4. Skip three lines and write your poem. Use some of the words from your list.

Edit

5. Reread your poem. Delete any words that don't fit. Add new words that will make your poem better.

6. Make sure each line begins with a capital letter and ends with a period.

Publish

7. Print your poem.

8. Share your poem with a friend.

9. Fill out the **Project Scorecard.**

UNIT 4

Drawing and Graphics

Graphics are pictures on the computer. They can be pictures that are drawn, or photos.

Stores use graphics in ads to sell things.

You can draw pictures on the computer to give to someone.

VIEW IT!

In this unit you will learn to use drawing and painting tools to create graphics.

Glossary

application also called a *program*; software designed to help the computer do specific activities, such as word processing

blank presentation a new file with no design or color

cable an electrical wire or bundle of wires used to connect two parts of a computer system

Caps Lock a key used to type all characters in upper case

CD-ROM a type of optical disk that is able to store large amounts of data

CD-ROM drive a device that can read information from a CD-ROM

cell the box formed at the point where a column and row meet in a spreadsheet or table

cell address the location (column letter and row number) of a cell in a spreadsheet

click to tap a mouse button, pressing down and then releasing it

clip art electronic pictures that can be added to documents

color palette a set of available colors

column items that go up and down on a page; columns in a spreadsheet are named A, B, C, and so on

command an instruction given to the computer

computer a machine that processes data, which can be words, numbers, or graphics, and can help organize, edit, and file information

cursor a pointer that shows the movement of the mouse

data information in the form of words, numbers, or graphics

electronic reference information that is stored on a CD-ROM or on the Internet, such as an encyclopedia or dictionary

Enter key a key that inserts a line break when tapped; called the *Return* key on a **Macintosh**

field one category of information in a database record

file also called a *document*; a page or pages created on a computer

Fill tool a paint tool used to fill an object with a color and/or pattern

floppy disk a removable storage device, usually one flat disk enclosed in a case; used to store small amounts of information

floppy disk drive the part of the computer used to read from or store information onto a floppy disk

folder an object used to organize information; it can contain files or other folders

font the style of text in a document

database a software program used to organize, find, and display information; any organized collection of information on a given subject or topic

delete to remove or erase

desktop a metaphor used to describe a file system as an office desktop; has pictures, called icons, that stand for drives, files, and folders

disk drive a machine that reads data from and writes data onto a disk

document also called a *file*; a page or pages created on a computer

double-click to tap a mouse button twice quickly

drag to move an object on the screen with the mouse while the button is held down

eject to take out

gadgets tools that connect to the computer to help do different things

graphic any computer-generated picture or image

hard drive a primary storage device, usually a stack of disks enclosed in a computer case, used to store large amounts of information; often called the "C" drive

hardware the physical parts of the computer system, such as the monitor, keyboard, and hard drive

Home Keys the keys A, S, D, F, J, K, L, and ; on a keyboard

home page a Web page that functions like the table of contents in a book to introduce a Web site

Home Row the "home" for fingers while keyboarding; the row on the keyboard that contains the keys A, S, D, F, J, K, L, and ;

I-beam the form of the cursor in a word processing document shaped like a capital I

icon a picture that represents a file or command on a computer display

input and output tools devices that connect to the computer that either put information into the computer or take it out

insertion point a mark that blinks on the screen to show the place where text will be inserted

Internet a huge network of computers that connects smaller networks of computers

keyboard a device that lets you talk with a computer; includes letters, numbers, symbols, and function keys

keyboarding typing on a computer

keys the buttons on a keyboard

key word a word used to help find information on a topic

layout the way things are placed on a file

log on the process of making a computer system or network recognize you so that you can begin a computer session

menu a list of commands or options from which you can choose

menu bar a menu that appears on top of a window; each item in a menu bar is a pull-down menu

monitor a display screen and the box that holds it

mouse a handheld input device used by rolling it over a flat surface, pointing, clicking, and dragging

mouse pad a pad on which to move a mouse; mouse pads make using the mouse easier

multimedia the use of more than one media, such as text, audio, video, and graphics, in a computer program

netiquette the basic rules to follow when writing electronic messages

network a system of computers linked together to share information and hardware

Page Down key often shortened PgDn; a key that usually scrolls the document down one full screen

Page Up key often shortened PgUp; a key that usually scrolls the document up one full screen

point to move the cursor, or pointer, to an item on a display screen

point size a unit of measure used for typeface sizes

presentation a show given for people

printer an output tool that gives information from the computer in printed form

program software that helps the computer do specific activities

record a group of fields that are related to the same topic or idea in a database

Return key a key that inserts a line break in a document when tapped; called the *Enter* key on a *PC* keyboard

row items that go from side to side on a page; rows in a spreadsheet are named *1, 2, 3,* and so on

scanner an input tool that puts words and pictures into the computer

screen short for *display screen;* the display part of a monitor

scroll bar a bar on the side or bottom of a window to control which part of a document is shown in the window

search engine a program that looks for word matches based on key words

select to highlight text in order to change it

Shift key a key used to change the meaning of other keys; used to form capital letters and symbols

slide an image made for use in a projector or viewer; may also be shown on a computer

slide show a series of slides given in a certain order

software a computer program that tells the computer what to do

Space Bar a long, horizontal key on the keyboard used to put spaces in a document

spreadsheet a computer program that works with numbers

Tab key a key used to move the insertion point to a preset position

text displayed or printed words, sentences, and paragraphs

title slide a slide that has a title and subtitle; tells what the slide show is about

toolbar the row of buttons near the top of an application window; clicking a toolbar button is a shortcut for choosing a command from a menu

undo to return to a previous state by undoing the effects of one or more commands

URL (Uniform Resource Locator) the location of a Web page that starts with the abbreviation http://

Web short for World Wide Web

Web browser software that allows the user to view and explore Internet Web pages

Web page an electronic page on the Internet that might have graphics, sound, and video clips; one page, or document, at a Web site

Web site all the Web pages, images, and other files of one person, company, or organization

window an enclosed rectangular area on a display screen

word processing the process of creating and editing documents

word wrap a word processing feature that automatically moves the insertion point to the next line when one line is filled with text

World Wide Web a system of Internet servers that supports specially formatted documents containing links, which allow the user to jump to other documents

Index

Boldface numbers refer to lesson numbers, unless pages are indicated.

A

Acceptable use policy, **2**, pages 5–6, 7

Airbrush tool, **34**

Alignment, 24

Alphabetic keys, **7–10**

Arrow keys, **4**, **19**, **29**, **42**, ...

Audio, **46**, **50**, pages 60, 75

B

Backspace key, **20**, **25**, **29**

Basic computer skills, *see* Computer basics

Blank document, **6**, **20**, **22**, **24**, **31–36**

Blank lines, **21**, **25**, **29**

Body position, *see* Posture

Browser, 49, 54

C

Cables, **1**

Capital letters, **22**

Caps lock, **7–10**, **13–18**, **20**, **22**

Case (upper and lower), **7–10**, **17**, **26**

CD-ROM, **2**, **45–48**, page 75

Cell, **41**, **42**, page 65

Cell address, **41**, page 65

Click, **3**, ...

Clip art, **39**, page 46

Close box, **5**

Close a file, **5**, **6**

Close a program, **6**

Color palette, **31**, **33–36**, **52**

Column, **41**, page 65

Communication, pages 7, 82

Computer, **1**, pages 1–7, ...
   history, pages 1–4
   parts, **1**
   rules, **2**
   safety and ethics, pages 5, 6

Computer basics, **1–6**, pages 7, 15

Create files, **6**, page 54

CPU, page 55

Cursor, **3**, ...

D

Data, **42**, **44**

Data input, **42**

Database, **43**, **44**, pages 70, 74

Delete key, **25**, **29**

Deleting text, **25**, **26**, **29**, **30**

Desktop, **3**, **21**, **27–29**, **38**, **39**

Digital camera, **37**, page 55

Digital information, **45**, **48**, **49**, **54**, pages 75, 82

Digital video, **51**

Disk drive, **1**, **2**, **45**

Document, **19**, ...

Double-click, **5**, **6**, **32**, **45**

Drag, **3**, **29**, **31**, **32**, **34–36**

Drawing, **31–36**, **52**, pages 46, 54

DVD, **45**, page 75

... skills practiced in multiple lessons

red indicates Teacher's Edition only

R7

E

Eject, **2**, **45–47**, page 81
Electronic reference, **45–48**, pages 75, 81
End key, **28**
Enter key, **4**, **14**, **21**, . . .
Entering text, **24**, **26**, **30**, . . .
Eraser tool, **31**, **35**
Ethics, **2**, pages 5–6, 7, 75
Exit programs, *see* Close a program

F

Field, **43**, page 74
File, **5**, **38**, *see also* Open a file, *see also* Close a file, . . .
Fill tool, **33**
Floppy disk drive, **2**
Font, **20–22**, **40**, page 30
Form, page 70
Format, **39**

G

Gadgets, **37**, **38**, pages 55, 59
Game, **47**, **53**, page 75
Go, **54**, page 90
Graph, page 65
Graphics, **31–36**, pages 46, 54

H

Handheld computer, **37**, page 55
Hand position, **13–18**
Hardware, **1**
Help, **50–54**
Highlighting, **29**, **30**
History, **1–4**
Home key, **28**, **30**
Home keys, **13–18**
Home page, **49**
Home row, **13–18**

I

I-beam, **19**
Icon, **3**, **5**, **6**, **45**, **46**
Input devices, **37**, page 55
Insertion point, **19**, **20**, **23–25**, **30**
Internet, **49–54**, pages 82, 90

J

Justification, **24**

K

Keyboard, **1**, **4**, **7–18**, **28**, **37**, pages 16, 55
Alphabetic keys, **7–10**
Home keys, **13–18**
Number keys, **11**, **12**
Symbol keys, **12**, **22**
Keyboarding, **7–18**, pages 16, 30, 31, 60
Key word search, **48**, page 81

L

Line tool, **36**
Links, page 90

M

Margin, **24**
Menu, **38**
Monitor, **1**, **37**
Mouse, **1**, **3**, . . .
Mouse pad, **3**
Multimedia, **39**, **40**, page 60

N

Name files, **6**, pages 54, 59, 64

Navigation, **4**, **19**, **28**, **42**, **44**, **49**, **52**

Network, pages 15, 82

New document, **6**, **31–36**

New lines, **14**, **21**, . . .

Number keys, **11**, **12**

O

Online, see Internet

Online help, **50–54**

Open a file, **5**, **6**, . . .

Open a program, **6**

Output devices, **37**, **38**, page 55

P

Page down key, **19**, **28**

Page up key, **19**, **28**, 30

Paintbrush tool, **31**

Painting, **34**, page 46

Pencil tool, **35**

Plagiarism, page 6

Policies, see Rules

Portfolio, **33**, pages 15, 30, 45, 54, 59, 64, 69, 74, 81, 90

Position, **13–18**

Posture, **9**, **10**, **13**, **17**, 18

Presentation software, **39**, **40**, pages 60, 64

Print preview, **38**

Printer, **1**, **37**, **38**, page 55

Printing, **30**, **38**, 52, . . .

Q

Quit, **6**, **45–47**

R

Record, **43**

Redo, **27**

Research tools, **48**

Return key, **14**, **21**, . . .

Row, **41**, pages 65, 69

Rules, **2**, pages 5, 6

Program, **6**, **31**, **52**, pages 31, 46, 60, 65, 70

Projects, pages 15, 30, 45, 54, 59, 64, 69, 74, 81, 90

Proofreading, page 45

Punctuation, **12**, **16**, page 45

S

Safety, **2**, pages 5, 6, 7, 82

Save files, **5**, **6**, **26**, pages 15, 30, 54, 59, 64, 69, 90

Scanner, **37**, page 55

Screen, 1

Scroll bar, **4**, **19**, **28**, **49**

Search, **48**, **52**

Select, **29**, **42**

Semicolon key, **16**

Shape tool, **32**, **33**, page 54

Shift key, **22**, **26**, **29**

Slide, **39**, **40**, pages 60, 64

Slide show, **39**, **40**, pages 60, 64

Software, pages 46, 65, 70

Sort, **43**

Space bar, **15**, . . .

Special keys, **28**

Spray can tool, **34**

Spreadsheet, **41**, **42**, pages 65, 69, 70

Start programs, *see* Open a program

Symbol keys, **12**, **22**

T

Tab, **23**, **42**, **44**

Tab key, **23**, **41**, **42**

Table, **43**, page 70

Text, **20**, . . .

Time, **18**

Title slide, **40**, page 64

Toolbar, **27**

Tools, **31–36**, **37**, **52**, page 54

Typing, **7–22**, page 16, *see also* Entering text, *see also* Keyboarding

U

Undo, **25**, **27**, **33**

URL, **49**, **54**, page 90

V

Video, **51**

View, **34**, **39**

W

Web, **49–54**, page 90

Web browser, **49**, **54**

Web page, **49**, **54**

Web site, **49**

White space, **31–34**, **36**, **40**, **52**

Word division, **18**, **24**

Word processing, **19–30**, pages 31, 45, 60

Word wrap, **24**

World Wide Web, **49**, *see also* Web

Wrap text, **24**

Z

Zoom, 31, 34

. . . skills practiced in multiple lessons   red indicates Teacher's Edition only

Mini-Manual

This Mini-Manual provides quick, step-by-step instruction for basic, frequently used technology tasks in *Microsoft Office* for *Windows XP* and *Macintosh OS X* and *AppleWorks* for *Macintosh*. The manual will also be invaluable to students who have mastered skills in one platform or program and are required to use another. Please note that the *Office* for *Macintosh* includes the programs *Word, Excel,* and *PowerPoint* but does not include the database program *Access.*

Major differences in program functionality are noted in the Mini-Manual. On *Macintosh* systems, for example, programs and files are closed on the left side of the window instead of on the right side, as in *Windows.* For more specific task, students should reference the appropriate lesson in *TechKnowledge.*

Task	MICROSOFT® OFFICE for Windows XP	MICROSOFT® OFFICE for Macintosh OS X	APPLEWORKS®
Align Text	1. Select the text to align. 2. Click the **Align Left, Center, Align Right,** or **Justify** button on the toolbar.	1. Select the text to align. 2. Click the **Align Left, Center, Align Right,** or **Justify** button on the toolbar.	1. Select the text to align. 2. Click the **Align Left, Center, Align Right,** or **Justify** button in the text ruler.
Bold	1. Select the text to bold. 2. Click the **Bold** button on the toolbar. **OR** 1. Click the **Bold** button on the toolbar. 2. Key the text to be in boldface. 3. Click the **Bold** button again.	1. Select the text to bold. 2. Click the **Bold** button on the toolbar. **OR** 1. Click the **Bold** button on the toolbar. 2. Key the text to be in boldface. 3. Click the **Bold** button again.	1. Select the text to bold. 2. Click the **Bold** icon on the button bar. **OR** 1. Click the **Bold** icon on the button bar. 2. Key the text to be in boldface. 3. Click the **Bold** icon again.

Task	MICROSOFT® OFFICE for Windows XP	MICROSOFT® OFFICE for Macintosh OS X	APPLEWORKS®
Bulleted and Numbered Lists	1. Click where the text should begin. 2. Click the **Bullets** or **Numbering** button on the toolbar. 3. Key the list. 4. Click the **Bullets** or **Numbering** button on the toolbar when finished.	1. Click where the text should begin. 2. Click the **Bullets** or **Numbering** button on the toolbar. 3. Key the list. 4. Click the **Bullets** or **Numbering** button on the toolbar when finished.	1. Click where the text should begin. 2. From the **Format** menu, choose **Paragraph.** 3. Select **Bullet** or **Numeric** from the **Label** drop-down box. Click **OK.** 4. Begin keying the list. When finished with the list, go back to **Paragraph** in the **Format** menu and select **None** from the **Label** box. You may have to adjust an automatic indent.
Clip Art—inserting	1. From the **Insert** menu, select **Picture,** then **Clip Art.** 2. On the **Clip Art** tab, click the category you want, select the desired image, and click the **Insert clip** button.	1. From the **Insert** menu, select **Picture,** then **Clip Art.** 2. On the **Clip Art** tab, click the category you want, select the desired image, and click the **Insert clip** button.	1. From the **File** menu, choose **Clippings.** 2. Select the clippings library you want to open. 3. Choose the desired clip art. 4. Double-click to insert the clip art.
Close—document	From the **File** menu, choose **Close,** or click the document's **Close** box (upper right corner).	From the **File** menu, choose **Close,** or click the document's **Close** box (upper left corner).	From the **File** menu, choose **Close,** or click the document's **Close Box** icon in the upper left corner of the document's title bar.
Close—program	Choose **Exit** from the file menu, or click the program's **Exit** box in the upper right corner.	From the **File** menu, choose **Quit.**	From the **AppleWorks** menu, choose **Quit AppleWorks.**
Copy	1. Select the text or cells to be copied.	1. Select the text or cells to be copied.	1. Select the text or cells to be copied.

Task	MICROSOFT® OFFICE for Windows XP	MICROSOFT® OFFICE for Macintosh OS X	APPLEWORKS®
Copy Files or Folders	2. From the **Edit** menu, choose **Copy,** or click the **Copy** button on the toolbar. 3. Position the cursor where you want the information to appear. 4. From the **Edit** menu, choose **Paste,** or click the **Paste** button on the toolbar. Drag the file or folder to be copied to the desired location. **OR** Use **Save As** from the **File** menu (see Save). **OR** Click on the file name or icon and select **Copy** and then **Paste** from the **Edit** menu.	2. From the **Edit** menu, choose **Copy,** or click the **Copy** button on the toolbar. 3. Position the cursor where you want the information to appear. 4. From the **Edit** menu, choose **Paste,** or click the **Paste** button on the toolbar. Drag the file or folder to be copied to the desired location. **OR** Use **Save As** from the File menu (see Save). **OR** Click on the file name or icon and select **Duplicate** from the **File** menu.	2. From the **Edit** menu, choose **Copy.** 3. Position the cursor where you want the information to appear. 4. From the **Edit** menu, choose **Paste.** Drag the file or folder to be copied to the desired location. **OR** Use **Copy** from the **File** menu, then **Paste** the item where it needs to be saved. **OR** Click on the file name or icon and select **Duplicate** from the **File** menu.
Cut and Paste	1. Select the text to be cut. 2. From the **Edit** menu, choose **Cut,** or click the **Cut** button on the toolbar. 3. Position the cursor where you want the information to appear. 4. From the **Edit** menu, choose **Paste,** or click the **Paste** button on the toolbar.	1. Select the text to be cut. 2. From the **Edit** menu, choose **Cut,** or click the **Cut** button on the toolbar. 3. Position the cursor where you want the information to appear. 4. From the **Edit** menu, choose **Paste,** or click the **Paste** button on the toolbar.	1. Select the text to be cut. 2. From the **Edit** menu, choose **Cut.** 3. Position the cursor where you want the information to appear. 4. From the **Edit** menu, choose **Paste.**
Database Forms— creating	1. From the **File** menu, choose **New.** 2. Click **OK** to the selection of a **Blank Database.**	1. From the **File** menu, choose **New.** 2. Click **OK** to the selection of a **Blank Database.**	1. From the **File** menu, choose **New.** 2. Select **Database** in the sub menu.

Task	MICROSOFT® OFFICE for Windows XP	MICROSOFT® OFFICE for Macintosh OS X	APPLEWORKS®
	3. In the **File New Database** dialog box, select the location in which to save the new database. Enter the file name for the new database. Click **Create.** 4. On the **Tables** tab, click **New.** Create a new table (see Database Tables—creating). When you are finished, the system returns you to the **Database** tabs. 5. On the **Forms** tab, click **New.** 6. Select **AutoForm: Columnar.** Underneath that, select the Table you created. Click **OK.** 7. When you close the form, the program will prompt you to save the form. It will be saved in the **Forms** tab.	3. In the **File New Database** dialog box, select the location in which to save the new database. Enter the file name for the new database. Click **Create.** 4. On the **Tables** tab, click **New.** Create a new table (see Database Tables—creating). When you are finished, the system returns you to the **Database** tabs. 5. On the **Forms** tab, click **New.** 6. Select **AutoForm: Columnar.** Underneath that, select the Table you created. Click **OK.** 7. When you close the form, the program will prompt you to save the form. It will be saved in the **Forms** tab.	3. In the **Field Name** box, type the field name. 4. In the **Field Type** box, select the type of field. Click **Create.** 5. Repeat steps 3 and 4 for each field. Click **Done.** 6. From the **Layout** menu, choose **Browse.**
Database Tables— creating	1. From the **File** menu, choose **New.** 2. Click **OK** to the selection of a **Blank Database.** 3. In the **File New Database** dialog box, select the location in which to save the new database. Enter the file name for the new database. Click **Create.** 4. On the **Tables** tab, click **New.** Select **Design View** and click **OK.**	1. From the **File** menu, choose **New.** 2. Click **OK** to the selection of a **Blank Database.** 3. In the **File New Database** dialog box, select the location in which to save the new database. Enter the file name for the new database. Click **Create.** 4. On the **Tables** tab, click **New.** Select **Design View** and click **OK.**	1. From the **File** menu, choose **New.** 2. Select **Database** in the sub menu. 3. In the **Field Name** box, type the field name. 4. In the **Field Type** box, select the type of field. Click **Create.** 5. Repeat steps 3 and 4 for each field. Click **Done.** 6. From the **Layout** menu, choose **List.**

Task	MICROSOFT® OFFICE for Windows XP	MICROSOFT® OFFICE for Macintosh OS X	APPLEWORKS®
	5. Enter a field name and choose a data type for each field. 6. Use the **View** menu to change to **Datasheet View.** 7. Click **Yes** to the prompt to save the table. 8. Name the table. Click **OK.** 9. A primary key is not necessary for elementary databases. Click **No.** 10. Enter the data in the table.	5. Enter a field name and choose a data type for each field. 6. Use the **View** menu to change to **Datasheet View.** 7. Click **Yes** to the prompt to save the table. 8. Name the table. Click **OK.** 9. A primary key is not necessary for elementary databases. Click **No.** 10. Enter the data in the table.	
Database Views— changing	For a table: From the **View** menu, choose the desired view—**Design View,** or **Datasheet View.** For a form: From the **View** menu, choose **Design View, Form View,** or **Datasheet View.**	For a table: From the **View** menu, choose the desired view—**Design View,** or **Datasheet View.** For a form: From the **View** menu, choose **Design View, Form View,** or **Datasheet View.**	From the **Layout** menu, choose the desired view—**Browse, Find, Layout,** or **List.**
Find and Replace	1. From the **Edit** menu, choose **Replace.** 2. In the **Find what** box, type the information to find. 3. In the **Replace with** box, type the replacement information. 4. Click **More** to select desired format options. 5. Choose the desired change button. 6. Close when finished.	1. From the **Edit** menu, choose **Replace.** 2. In the **Find what** box, type the information to find. 3. In the **Replace with** box, type the replacement information. 4. Click **More** to select desired format options. 5. Choose the desired change button. 6. Close when finished.	1. From the **Edit** menu, choose **Find/Change.** 2. Choose **Find/Change** again from the submenu. 3. Type the information to find in the **Find** box. 4. Type the replacement information in the **Change** box. 5. Select the desired find options. 6. Click the appropriate change button. 7. Close the **Find/Change** box when finished.

Task	MICROSOFT® OFFICE for Windows XP	MICROSOFT® OFFICE for Macintosh OS X	APPLEWORKS®
Find Files or Folders	1. Click the **Start** button. Choose **Search** and then **For Files or Folders.** 2. On the **Search Results** page, type the file name in the **Search for files or folders named** box. 3. In the **Look in** box, click the arrow to select the location to search. 4. Click **Search Now** to browse the location. 5. Click **Stop Search** to stop searching. 6. Double-click on the file or folder in the **Search Results** window.	1. From the Desktop, choose **Find** in the **File** menu. 2. In the **Find File** dialog box, select the location in which to search for the file and the file name. 3. Click **Find.**	1. From the Desktop, choose **Find** in the **File** menu. 2. In the **Search in** dialog box, select the location in which to search for the file. 3. Type the file name in the **File Name** box. 4. Click **Search.**
Folders—creating	1. In the folder location in which you want to place a new folder, choose **New** from the **File** menu, then **Folder.** A new folder appears. 2. Type a name for the folder and press the Enter key. **OR** Click the right mouse button and select **New** and then **Folder** from the pop-up menu.	1. From the Desktop drive, click **New Folder** from the **File** menu. A new, highlighted folder appears. 2. Type a name for the folder and press the Return key. **OR** Click the right mouse button and select **New** and then **Folder** from the pop-up menu.	1. From the Desktop drive, click **New Folder** in the **File** menu. A new, highlighted folder appears. 2. Type a name for the folder and press the Return key.
Font—changing typeface and size	1. From the **Format** menu, select **Font.** 2. Select the **Font** tab. 3. Choose a typeface from the options in the **Font** box.	1. From the **Format** menu, select **Font.** 2. Select the **Font** tab. 3. Choose a typeface from the options in the **Font** box.	To change a typeface, select the **Font** menu in the text ruler, drag to the desired font, and release. To change a font size, select the

Level 1 • Mini-Manual

Task	MICROSOFT® OFFICE for Windows XP	MICROSOFT® OFFICE for Macintosh OS X	APPLEWORKS®
Graphics—selecting	4. Choose a font size from the options in the **Size** box. 5. Click **OK.** In *Word,* place the mouse pointer over the graphic and click once. In *Paint,* use the Select tool.	4. Choose a font size from the options in the **Size** box. 5. Click **OK.** In *Word,* place the mouse pointer over the graphic and click once. In *Paint,* use the Select tool.	**Size** menu in the text ruler, drag to the desired size, and release. In a word processing document, place the mouse pointer over the graphic and click once. In a paint document, use the Select tool.
Graphs—converting spreadsheet data to graphs	1. Select the range of cells to include in the chart. 2. Click the **Chart Wizard** button on the toolbar, or select **Chart** from the **Insert** menu. 3. In the **Standard Types** tab, select a chart type, and click **Next.** 4. Click **Next** again to change chart options such as title, axis labels, and appearance. Use the tabs along the top. 5. Click **Finish.**	1. Select the range of cells to include in the chart. 2. Click the **Chart Wizard** button on the toolbar, or select **Chart** from the **Insert** menu. 3. In the **Standard Types** tab, select a chart type, and click **Next.** 4. Click **Next** again to change chart options such as title, axis labels, and appearance. Use the tabs along the top. 5. Click **Finish.**	1. Select the range of cells to include in the chart. 2. From the **Options** menu, choose **Make Chart.** 3. Select a chart type from the **Gallery.** 4. Under **Modify,** click the other buttons to change chart options, such as the labels, title, and appearance of the graph. 5. Click **OK.**
Headers and Footers	In *Word:* 1. From the **View** menu, choose **Header and Footer.** A header box and a **Header and Footer** toolbar appears. 2. Choose the header or footer, using the **Switch Between Header and Footer** toolbar button.	In *Word:* 1. From the **View** menu, choose **Header and Footer.** A header box and a **Header and Footer** toolbar appears. 2. Choose the header or footer, using the **Switch Between Header and Footer** toolbar button.	1. From the **Format** menu, choose **Insert Header** or **Insert Footer.** 2. Key the desired text and apply any desired formatting. 3. Click in the text area when finished. Once the header or footer appears in the document, you can easily

Task	MICROSOFT® OFFICE for Windows XP	MICROSOFT® OFFICE for Macintosh OS X	APPLEWORKS®
	3. Key the desired text and apply any desired formatting. 4. Click **Close** on the **Header and Footer** toolbar when finished. In **Print Layout** or **Page Layout** View, you can click in the header or footer and key text. In *Excel:* 1. Select **Header and Footer** in the **View** menu. 2. In the **Header/Footer** tab, click **Custom Header** or **Custom Footer.** 3. Key text and click **OK.**	3. Key the desired text and apply any desired formatting. 4. Click **Close** on the **Header and Footer** toolbar when finished. In **Print Layout** or **Page Layout** View, you can click in the header or footer and key text. In *Excel:* 1. Select **Header and Footer** in the **View** menu. 2. In the **Header/Footer** tab, click **Custom Header** or **Custom Footer.** 3. Key text and click **OK.**	change the text, page numbers, and other contents by clicking in the header or footer area.
Help	1. From the **Help** menu, choose the help option for the program being used. 2. Click the **Index** tab. 3. Key a descriptive word for the action or item you want information about in Box 1. 4. Click the desired topic in Box 2. 5. Press Return or Enter.	1. From the **Help** menu, choose **Contents and Index.** 2. Click the **Index** button, and then navigate through the index by clicking on the letters and topics in the left-hand column. 3. Click the arrow next to the major topic to display a list of subtopics. 4. Click the desired subtopic.	1. From the **Help** menu, choose **AppleWorks Help.** 2. Type the keyword(s) in the search box and click **Ask.** 3. Select the desired topic from the list in the left-hand column.
Margins	1. From the **File** menu, choose **Page Setup.** 2. Choose the **Margins** tab. 3. Key or select the desired margin widths in the margin boxes. 4. Click **OK.**	1. From the **File** menu, choose **Page Setup.** In *Word:* Click the arrow to change the first box to *Microsoft Word,* if necessary. In *Excel:* Click the **Margins** tab.	1. From the **Format** menu, choose **Document.** 2. Key the desired margin widths in the **Margin** boxes. 3. Click **OK.**

Task	MICROSOFT® OFFICE for Windows XP	MICROSOFT® OFFICE for Macintosh OS X	APPLEWORKS®
New Document	From the **File** menu, choose **New**.	From the **File** menu, choose **New**.	1. From the **File** menu, choose **New**. 2. Select a document type.
	2. Press the **Margin** button. 3. Key or select the desired margin widths in the margin boxes. 4. Click **OK**.		
Open a File	1. From the **File** menu, choose **Open**. 2. Change directories, if necessary, by clicking the arrow next to the **Look in** box. 3. Select a document from the list and click **Open**.	1. From the **File** menu, choose **Open**. 2. Change directories, if necessary, by clicking the arrow next to the current folder or drive under the **Name** box. 3. Select a document from the list and click **Open**.	1. From the **File** menu, choose **Open**. 2. Change directories, if necessary, by using the folder icons to find the desired folder. 3. Select a document from the list and click **Open**.
Presentation—add a slide transition	1. Choose **Slide Sorter** from the **View** menu. Select the slide or slides to add transitions to. 2. Select **Slide Transition** from the **Slide Show** menu. 3. Choose a transition type and speed in the **Effect** box. Add a sound and change the transition advance prompt in using the **Sound** and **Advance** boxes. 4. Click **Apply** to apply the transition to the selected slide, and click **Apply to All** to apply the transition to all the slides in the presentation.	1. Choose **Slide Sorter** from the **View** menu. Select the slide or slides to add transitions to. 2. Select **Slide Transition** from the **Slide Show** menu. 3. Choose a transition type and speed in the **Effect** box. Add a sound and change the transition advance prompt in using the **Sound** and **Advance** boxes. 4. Click **Apply** to apply the transition to the selected slide, and click **Apply to All** to apply the transition to all the slides in the presentation.	1. Click the **Slide** tab in the **Controls** window. 2. Select a slide you want a transition before. 3. Select a transition from the pull-down menu in the **Slide** panel of the **Controls** window. If you do not see the **Controls** window, choose **Show Presentation Controls** from the **Window** menu.

Task	MICROSOFT® OFFICE for Windows XP	MICROSOFT® OFFICE for Macintosh OS x	APPLEWORKS®
Presentation—change a slide layout	1. From the **Normal** or **Slide Sorter** views, select the slide or slides you want to change. 2. Choose **Slide Layout** from the **Format** menu. 3. Choose a slide layout from the **Autolayout** box and click **Apply.** 4. Edit the slide to fit the new layout.	1. From the **Normal** or **Slide Sorter** views, select the slide or slides you want to change. 2. Choose **Slide Layout** from the **Format** menu. 3. Choose a slide layout from the **Autolayout** box and click **Apply.** 4. Edit the slide to fit the new layout.	1. Click the **Slide** tab in the **Controls** window. 2. Select the slide that you want to edit. 3. Add, rearrange, and edit the content and layout of the slide. If you do not see the **Controls** window, choose **Show Presentation Controls** from the **Window** menu.
Presentation—changing views	From the **View** menu, click **Normal, Slide Sorter, Notes Page,** or **Slide Show.** **OR** Click the **Normal, Slide Sorter, Notes Page,** or **Slide Show** button in the lower left-hand corner of the *PowerPoint* window.	From the **View** menu, click **Normal, Slide Sorter, Notes Page,** or **Slide Show.** **OR** Click the **Normal, Slide Sorter, Notes Page,** or **Slide Show** button in the lower left-hand corner of the *PowerPoint* window.	From the **Window** menu, choose **Notes View** or **Slide Show.**
Presentation—new presentation	1. From the **File** menu, choose **New,** or click the **New** button on the toolbar. 2. Choose a design for the new presentation or create a blank presentation. Click **OK.** 3. Choose a slide layout from the **Autolayout** box and click **OK.** Enter text on the new slide. 4. Click the **New Slide** button on the toolbar or select **New Slide** from the **Insert** menu. 5. Repeat steps 3 and 4 for each new slide.	1. From the **File** menu, choose **New,** or click the **New** button on the toolbar. 2. Choose a design for the new presentation or create a blank presentation. Click **OK.** 3. Choose a slide layout from the **Autolayout** box and click **OK.** Enter text on the new slide. 4. Click the **New Slide** button on the toolbar or select **New Slide** from the **Insert** menu. 5. Repeat steps 3 and 4 for each new slide.	1. From the **File** menu, choose **New.** 2. Select **Presentation** from the **New** menu.

Task	MICROSOFT® OFFICE for Windows XP	MICROSOFT® OFFICE for Macintosh OS X	APPLEWORKS®
Presentation—new slide	1. In the **View** menu, select **Normal.** 2. In the outline pane on the left-hand side of the screen, select the slide after which you want the new slide to appear. 3. Click the **New Slide** button on the toolbar or select **New Slide** from the **Insert** menu. 4. Choose a slide layout from the **Autolayout** box and click **OK.**	1. In the **View** menu, select **Normal.** 2. In the outline pane on the left-hand side of the screen, select the slide after which you want the new slide to appear. 3. Click the **New Slide** button on the toolbar or select **New Slide** from the **Insert** menu. 4. Choose a slide layout from the **Autolayout** box and click **OK.**	1. Click the **Slide** tab in the **Controls** window. 2. Click the **Plus** (+) button. If you do not see the **Controls** window, choose **Show Presentation Controls** from the **Window** menu.
	6. To save the presentation, select **Save** from the **File** menu. Enter a name in the **File name** box, then click **Save.**	6. To save the presentation, select **Save** from the **File** menu. Enter a name in the **File name** box, then click **Save.**	
Presentation—view a slide show	Select **Slide Show** from the **View** menu. **OR** Click on the **Slide Show** button in the lower left-hand corner of the *PowerPoint* window.	Select **Slide Show** from the **View** menu. **OR** Click on the **Slide Show** button in the lower left-hand corner of the *PowerPoint* window.	Select **Slide Show** from the **Window** menu. **OR** Click the **Slide Show** tab in the **Controls** window, and then click the **Play** button. If you do not see the **Controls** window, choose **Show Presentation Controls** from the **Window** menu.
Print	Click the **Print** button on the toolbar. **OR** 1. From the **File** menu, choose **Print.** 2. Change the settings as desired.	Click the **Print** button on the toolbar. **OR** 1. From the **File** menu, choose **Print.** 2. Change the settings as desired.	Click the **Print** button on the button bar. **OR** 1. From the **File** menu, choose **Print.** 2. Change the settings as desired.

Task	MICROSOFT® OFFICE for Windows XP	MICROSOFT® OFFICE for Macintosh OS X	APPLEWORKS®
	3. Click **OK** or **Print.**	3. Click **OK** or **Print.**	3. Click **OK** or **Print.**
Resave	From the **File** menu, choose **Save,** or click the **Save** button on the toolbar.	From the **File** menu, choose **Save,** or click the **Save** button on the toolbar.	From the **File** menu, choose **Save,** or click the **Save** button on the toolbar.
Save	1. From the **File** menu, choose **Save As.** 2. Choose a location to save to in the **Save in** box. 3. Type a document name in the **File name** box. 4. Click **Save.**	1. From the **File** menu, choose **Save As.** 2. Choose a location in which to save. 3. Type a document name. 4. Click **Save.**	1. From the **File** menu, choose **Save As.** 2. Choose a location in which to save. 3. Type a document name. 4. Click **Save.**
Select Text	1. To select one or more characters, click in front of the first character and drag the mouse over the text. 2. To select an entire document, from the **Edit** menu, choose **Select All.** 3. To select a word, double-click it.	1. To select one or more characters, click in front of the first character and drag the mouse over the text. 2. To select an entire document, from the **Edit** menu, choose **Select All.** 3. To select a word, double-click it.	1. To select one or more characters, click in front of the first character and drag the mouse over the text. 2. To select an entire document, from the **Edit** menu, choose **Select All.** 3. To select a word, double-click it.
Spelling Checker	Click the **Spelling Checker** button on the toolbar.	Click the **Spelling Checker** button on the toolbar.	Click the **Spelling Checker** button on the button bar.
Spreadsheet Columns and Rows— inserting and deleting	To insert a column or row: 1. Click the column letter or row number before which you want to insert a column or row. 2. From the **Insert** menu, choose **Columns** or **Rows.** To delete a selected column or row: from the **Edit** menu, select **Delete.**	To insert a column or row: 1. Click the column letter or row number before which you want to insert a column or row. 2. From the **Insert** menu, choose **Columns** or **Rows.** To delete a selected column or row: from the **Edit** menu, select **Delete.**	To insert a column or row: 1. Click the column letter or row number before which you want to insert a column or row. 2. From the **Format** menu, choose **Insert Cells.** To delete a selected column or row: from the **Format** menu, click **Delete Cells.**

Task	MICROSOFT® OFFICE for Windows XP	MICROSOFT® OFFICE for Macintosh OS X	APPLEWORKS®
Spreadsheet Formulas—entering	1. Click the cell to contain the formula. 2. Type = to begin the formula. 3. Type a formula, including cell references and mathematical operators, such as +, -, *, or /. 4. Press Enter or Return.	1. Click the cell to contain the formula. 2. Type = to begin the formula. 3. Type a formula, including cell references and mathematical operators, such as +, -, *, or /. 4. Press Enter or Return.	1. Click the cell to contain the formula. 2. Type = to begin the formula. 3. Type a formula, including cell references and mathematical operators, such as +, -, *, or /. 4. Press Enter or Return.
Spreadsheet Functions—entering	1. Click the cell where the function result (SUM, AVERAGE, MAXIMUM) should appear. 2. For Sum, type =SUM(Cell Reference:Cell Reference) 3. For Average, type =AVG(Cell Reference:Cell Reference) Example: =SUM(A3:A6) 4. For Maximum, type =MAX(Cell Reference:Cell Reference) 5. Press Return or Enter.	1. Click the cell where the function result (SUM, AVERAGE, MAXIMUM) should appear. 2. For Sum, type =SUM(Cell Reference:Cell Reference) 3. For Average, type =AVG(Cell Reference:Cell Reference) Example: =SUM(A3:A6) 4. For Maximum, type =MAX(Cell Reference:Cell Reference) 5. Press Return or Enter.	1. Click the cell where the function result (SUM, AVERAGE, MAXIMUM) should appear. 2. For Sum, type =SUM(Cell Reference:Cell Reference) 3. For Average, type =AVG(Cell Reference:Cell Reference) Example: =SUM(A3:A6) 4. For Maximum, type =MAX(Cell Reference:Cell Reference) 5. Press Return or Enter.
Spreadsheets—filling	1. Select the cell(s) to be copied and all cells in the direction (down, up, left, right) to fill. 2. From the **Edit** menu, choose **Fill**, and then click the desired direction. 3. To fill with a series of numbers, dates, or times, select the starting cell and the range of cells to fill. From the **Edit** menu, click **Fill**, and then click **Series.** Choose the desired options, then click **OK.**	1. Select the cell(s) to be copied and all cells in the direction (down, up, left, right) to fill. 2. From the **Edit** menu, choose **Fill**, and then click the desired direction. 3. To fill with a series of numbers, dates, or times, select the starting cell and the range of cells to fill. From the **Edit** menu, click **Fill**, and then click **Series.** Choose the desired options, then click **OK.**	1. Select the cell(s) to be copied and all cells in the direction (down or right) to fill. 2. From the **Calculate** menu, choose the appropriate Fill direction. 3. To fill with a series of numbers, dates, or times, select the starting cell and the range of cells to fill. From the **Calculate** menu, choose **Fill Special.** Choose the desired options, then click **OK.**

Task	MICROSOFT® OFFICE for Windows XP	MICROSOFT® OFFICE for Macintosh OS X	APPLEWORKS®
Tab Set	1. From the **Format** menu, choose **Tabs.** 2. In the **Tab stop position** box, type the position of the tab (such as 0.5 in). 3. Select an alignment. 4. Under **Leader,** choose **None** or choose the desired leader, and click **Set.** 5. Click **OK** when finished.	1. From the **Format** menu, choose **Tabs.** 2. In the **Tab stop position** box, type the position of the tab (such as 0.5 in). 3. Select an alignment. 4. Under **Leader,** choose **None** or choose the desired leader, and click **Set.** 5. Click **OK** when finished.	1. From the **Format** menu, click **Tabs.** 2. Select an option from the **Alignment** box. 3. Type a position in the **Position** box. 4. Click **OK.** 5. To move a tab, drag it to a new position on the text ruler.
Tables and Spreadsheets—adjusting column width or row height	1. Move the cursor to the cell border. 2. When the cursor changes to a crosshair pointer, click and drag the cell boundary.	1. Move the cursor to the cell border. 2. When the cursor changes to a crosshair pointer, click and drag the cell boundary.	From the **Format** menu, select **Column Width** or **Row Height.** **OR** 1. Move the cursor to the cell border. 2. When the cursor changes to a crosshair pointer, click and drag the cell boundary.
Tables—inserting	1. From the **Table** menu, choose **Insert,** then **Table.** 2. Select the number of desired rows and columns. 3. Click **OK.** 4. Click in a cell, key text, and press the Tab key to move to the next cell.	1. From the **Table** menu, choose **Insert,** then **Table.** 2. Select the number of desired rows and columns. 3. Click **OK.** 4. Click in a cell, key text, and press the Tab key to move to the next cell.	1. From the **Table** menu, choose **Insert Table.** 2. Select the number of desired rows and columns. 3. Click **OK.** 4. Click in a cell, key text, and then click in the next cell.
Toolbars—viewing	From the **View** menu, choose **Toolbars** and click the desired toolbar.	From the **View** menu, choose **Toolbars** and click the desired toolbar.	From the **Window** menu, choose **Show Tools** or **Show Button Bar.**